CORPORATE
FREE AGENCY

7 Principles Toward
Career Ownership

Brandon Shelby

ISBN 979-8-88943-510-5 (paperback)
ISBN 979-8-88943-511-2 (digital)

Christian Faith Publishing
832 Park Avenue
Meadville, PA 16335
www.christianfaithpublishing.com

Special Thanks to, Will Utley
for the photographs.
https://www.willutleyphotography.com/

Printed in the United States of America

To people who still have a dream, you have everything you need to be great.

Commit your works to the Lord and your thoughts will be established. A man's Heart plans his way, but the Lord directs his steps.

—Proverbs 16:3, 9

CONTENTS

PREFACE AND MISSION STATEMENT

CORPORATE FREE AGENCY
7 Principles Toward
Career Ownership

The mission of *Corporate Free Agency* is to educate and empower individuals to take ownership of their professional lives through faith, proper planning, preparation, and action, thus producing positive results.

ACKNOWLEDGMENTS

Special acknowledgments are in order as I want to thank my friends and family for all their support.

My parents, James and Lorna Shelby, for your unconditional love and support.

My friend and fraternity brother, Dr. Charles Dorsey, for passing along the vision that I could be a writer too through the 10-Day eBook Challenge.

To my brothers, Arnold Randall and William Utley, your artistic vision and creativity know no bounds. Thank you for bringing the visual aspect of *Corporate Free Agency* to life.

To my amazing daughters, Olivia and Layla—you are beautiful, you are smart, you are strong, you are brave, and you can do anything in Jesus's name. Amen.

To my inspiration and my rock, my wife, Audrey Shelby, we can do anything through Christ, who strengthens us. I love you, and the best is yet to come, my love.

INTRODUCTION

Corporate free agency is a term used to describe the growing trend of employees leaving their current jobs for new jobs or perhaps they are leaving to start their own businesses. This trend is being driven by several factors, including the increasing availability of technology and the desire for more flexibility and work autonomy.

But what does it really mean to be a corporate free agent?

Simply put, a corporate free agent is someone who has taken ownership over their careers.

Many people dream of making the leap from employee to manager, manager to executive, or executive to entrepreneur. The benefits can be enormous—more control over your time, greater clarity over your career trajectory, and the ability to make a real difference in the world by doing what you love most.

This new breed of worker is often highly skilled and highly sought after, and they are changing the way businesses look for talent.

CHAPTER 1

—〰—

Why Are You Looking to Make a Move?

My corporate career started back in 2004, circa 2006, at Macy's Federated, working as an HR assistant manager—which was a fancy title for human resources coordinator. I worked between two stores in Brea and Montebello, which happened to be primary locations for the region at that time, helping with some recruiting, but my main responsibility was doing the grunt work literally from setting up the orientation room each week when we had new hires, assisting with onboarding paperwork, filing paperwork, and creating tracking systems to help quantify results. Keep in mind that I had previous work experience that prepared me for this moment through college. I had rewarding summer internships through a nonprofit organization called INROADS. "The Mission of INROADS is to deliver innovative leadership development programs and creative solutions that identify, accelerate and elevate underrepresented talent throughout their careers" (I highly recommend this program to all young people looking for paid internships, apply today in inroads.org/apply).

My host companies were ADT Security Services and Pfizer Pharmaceuticals where I spent three consecutive summers working from 2002 through 2005—gaining invaluable work experience and developing my soft skills from a professional standpoint. I would not be here today if it were not for INROADS and the staff that poured into me. I mention this to help set the context and present my humble beginnings because I need you to understand why I made my initial move as a corporate free agent; the pure and unbridled motivator was money! In 2005, As a recent graduate of Cal Poly Pomona University with a degree in business administration with an emphasis in human resources with three consecutive years of internship experience working for two Fortune 500 organizations, here I was making $29,000 a year. Oh, did I mention I was living at home with my parents as a recent grad and young adult? I had friends buying homes and making money in real estate during the housing market boom, and I did not have enough to get my own apartment at the time.

My decision to leave Macy's Federated was based on a desire to want more out of a career than what I was getting, I wanted more money, but the core reason for my decision was rooted in emotion and insecurity. Looking back at that time now, I never had a conversation with my manager at Macy's about my career aspirations. I did not ask her about her plans for me and where she saw my career going as a result of my performance to that point. Moreover, I never sought the guidance of my friend and mentor, who helped me get the opportunity to compete for the position at Macy's in the first place (to whom I am forever indebted as well). You see, as a corporate free agent, you must ask yourself some key questions. Check your ego at the door because you are making a business decision that affects the trajectory of your career:

- Why do I want to leave my current organization?

- Do I have the support and band-width to grow here?
- Leaving means you are starting all over again—are you prepared to do that?
- Have you weighed all your options? Pros and cons?
- Have you exhausted, taken advantage of, and looked into all opportunities at your current organization before you decided to leave?
- Are you prepared for this new opportunity? Professionally, personally, spiritually, mentally, and physically?
- Are you making this decision based upon your emotions, or are you feeling compelled or almost a "called" to something more? Something greater?

As a corporate free agent, asking these questions along with doing the work behind the scenes day in and day out will help you make informed decisions throughout your career. Much like professional athletes that we idolize today—you must think of opportunities from a symbiotic approach: What's in it for me? How can I add value to this organization?

- Values
- Company culture
- Mission and vision
- Diversity, equity, and inclusion makeup
- Leadership structure
- Five- to ten- to twenty-year strategic plan
- Are there pay equity initiatives?
- What do their benefits look like?
- Technology and innovation

- Are the people you are speaking with happy to be there?

  o What made them join this orga-
    nization?
  o What has kept them there
    regardless of length and ten-
    ure at the organization?

As a reminder, I am giving you the guidelines and blueprint on what to think about when considering your next career. It is up to you to properly plan, prepare, and meditate on what you want; manifest all you want but put the work behind it.

CHAPTER 2

———〰———

What Makes You Special?

*Looking back so the view looking
forward is clearer.*

—Unknown

According to Zippia's *The Career Expert* written by Jack Flynn, published May 4, 2022,

> 18 Great Resignation Statistics 2022: Why are Americans leaving their jobs?

How many people quit their jobs in 2021? *47 million Americans left their jobs in 2021*. With an average of 3.98 million leaving their jobs every single month, peaking in November when 4.5 million people quit. For context, this all means that 23.5% of the total U.S. workforce resigned from their jobs in 2021.

I share these stats to ask the question of what makes you different or special from the millions of other Americans that have left their jobs for new opportunities.

Self-evaluation is critical here. We must be honest with ourselves about what makes us special, what sets us apart from the competition, and why someone should buy into our brand. You do realize that you are a brand "manager"? A brand manager is defined as a person responsible for supervising the promotion of a particular brand of goods. You are the "brand," and you have the "goods." There are many tools out there that can help identify your core strengths and areas of opportunity to improve such as the Myers-Briggs Type Indicator, true colors, enneagram of personality, and the DISC assessment. There is no better tool than to look in the mirror and be honest with your shortcomings, your flaws, and your weaknesses. It's not enough to acknowledge your shortcomings but take action to correct some of those shortcomings. How do you expect to manage your brand if you are not honest with yourself?

CORPORATE FREE AGENCY

I encourage each of you to ask some strength-based questions; here are a few examples below:

1. What has been working well for me in my career thus far?
2. What can I do better to improve professionally and personally?
3. What do I value most about myself?
4. If people could describe me in one word, what word would that be and why?

This is a shorter chapter, but it is an impactful one because you must do the work! If you have not done so before, I encourage you to journal, make a vision board, and set tangible goals and timelines that you plan to reach those goals. Put your plan into action and do the work! Failure to plan means that you are planning to fail; you have all the tools you need at your disposal, use what you have, and do all you can with what you have. There is a favorite character of mine in the Bible referenced in the book of Judges 3:31, Shamgar, "After Ehud, Shamgar son of Anath *rescued* Israel. He killed 600 Philistines with an ox goad." There is no more mention of Shamgar anywhere else in the Bible. His exploits and accomplishments were only worth one verse apparently; in fact, out of the 31,102 verses included in all sixty-six books of the Bible starting with Genesis to Revelation, there is only one verse mention of Shamgar—who was this leader, this king, prime minister, and this judge who presided over the people of Israel? Well, based on this one impactful verse, we can extract and see that Shamgar was first and foremost

(1) a leader,
(2) wise enough to preside as judge over the people,

(3) a hero that rescued the people of Israel, and

(4) did the work that was assigned to him.

Some of you want to advance your career, step into leadership roles, become entrepreneurs, and get your just due—but have you completed your current assignment with satisfactory or above average results? What makes you special and unique in this season, and how are you going to grow to get to the next level?

I encourage you to do the work, and your work will speak for itself; as you can see with Shamgar, all you need is one mention of your accomplishments to be deemed great and worthy of mention. Do the work; good people do the work.

CHAPTER 3

Are You in Alignment?

Webster's Dictionary defines *alignment* as "(1) *the act of aligning or state of being aligned* especially the proper positioning or state of adjustment of parts (as of a mechanical or electronic device) in relation to each other, (2a) a forming in line, (b) the line thus formed."

True story: one Sunday evening, my wife, two daughters, and I are at my parents' house for Sunday dinner like we normally do. After dinner, we watched football, and my wife was busy doing Layla's our three-year-old daughter's hair, and my oldest daughter, age six, was bored, so my wife suggested we go outside and play. My oldest daughter, Olivia, and I go out to the backyard to play catch. Now early on in this exchange of playing catch, my baby was not catching the ball with her hands, and she kept using her body to secure the ball and, in the process, leaving herself open to being hit in the head. So I encouraged her to keep her eye on the ball, attack it, and catch it with her hands; I gave her these instructions all while having my phone in my left hand—checking my fantasy football results. Olivia started catching the ball, and we were both excited about her progress; her confidence grew in a short amount of time.

I did all this quality coaching while still trying to check the day's stats; after about five exchanges going back and forth, I started noticing Olivia holding up her left hand and staring in between catching the ball.

This eventually caught my attention, and I asked her, "Baby, what are you doing?" as I was about to toss the ball back to her, and she replied, looking at her hand, "Looking at my phone."

My heart sank; she looked up at me with those hazel eyes, and her left hand propped as if she were holding a phone; that look said to me, "Do you see me now, Dad? Can you be present with me now and play catch without distractions?" I immediately put my phone down, walked over to my daughter, picked her up, hugged her, and told her, "I hear you. I'm sorry. I hear you. Let's play." I put her down, and we commenced to play catch without distractions. Being in alignment means being present where you are currently in your career.

CORPORATE FREE AGENCY

In an age where we are prone to mimic what is being presented on Instagram, Facebook, LinkedIn, TikTok, etc;. it is imperative for you to master the position and field you currently find yourself in. There will always be distractions—for example, new job opportunities being posted daily on LinkedIn or Indeed and updates of connections on LinkedIn receiving new promotional job opportunities. In 2021, we saw unprecedented movement during the "great resignation," where in some cases, individuals moved two to three times in less than a year before landing with a company and/or a position that they felt aligned with their objectives professionally. Financial gain will always be the top driving force to entertain new career opportunities, but in the world of corporate free agency, you must look at the full picture.

As you consider whether you are in alignment or not, ask the following:

1. Understanding the values of an organization? Have them define them for you!
2. What's the general makeup of an organization?
3. Are the reviews about an organization and its leadership positive or negative?
4. You should be able to identify yourself in that organization through its values, mission statement, and/or principles.
5. Do not be afraid to fail; you only fail when you do not attempt to try at all!

Finally, network, network, and network some more! The saying "Your network will determine your net worth" is so true. You will be amazed at how far and how wide your network can reach when you take stock of who is in your network and where they are from a professional standpoint.

CHAPTER 4

Be Intentional!

Keep your eyes on the ball, not on the Birdies!

—Olivia Shelby

The hardest part about making career moves is the intentional effort that it takes to move forward. Intentionality takes a certain level of drive and initiative to execute a plan that is critical to the success of anyone attempting to reach the goals that you set forth. James Baker, former United States

Secretary of State, said, "Proper preparation prevents poor performance." In my profession, I speak with people all the time, and you would be surprised that unfortunately, some get an interview, and they are not prepared. In certain cases, individuals are ill-equipped or unprepared to answer questions about themselves. This does not mean that they are not qualified or they do not have the experience to advance to the next level; in fact, they have shown a desire to test the "free agent" market by applying to a position. When I call candidates to inquire about their experience, understanding of the position, and what their desired salary expectation is, most lack the awareness or confidence to speak about themselves in a manner that tells me they are confident in their ability and that they know their worth. I am not limiting worth to salary and total compensation; ask yourself the following:

- What conditions are you willing to work under?
- What are some core must-haves an employer should possess to retain your talent?
- Is your preference to work remotely or in person?
- Do you want to manage people? If so, how do you see yourself leading others?
- What is your bottom line? Salary, bonus, and total compensation and benefits?

An intentional approach means that you already have a plan and you are prepared to

(1) take action and
(2) execute.

Taking intentional action means that you must *think*, *function*, and *focus*. Let me break these principles down further. Think about the task that is at hand and meditate on what you are trying to accomplish. Functioning amidst the chaos of the day, you getting to the next level does not mean you are absolved of your current responsibilities. You still have a job today; you must still produce at a high level and, believe it or not, how you finish your current position dictates how you start your next opportunity. Finally, focus on the goal, which is to transition into your next opportunity. *Corporate Free Agency* is built upon the premise of beginning with the end in mind. Keep your eye on the ball, and do not be distracted by what others are doing; you have your own journey, and your victory/success will come when you take ownership over your career.

CHAPTER 5

—⚏—

Know Your Worth!

Knowing your worth has a lot to do with understanding the urgency of now. In today's corporate world, procrastination can be detrimental and stifling to your professional growth. Yes, unemployment is at record lows, 3.4 percent to be exact (Bureau of Labor stats by United States Department of Labor), in this inflated market, you must act. Nothing is going to be given to you; you must state what you are worth and hold true to that statement. Others around you, leadership and coworkers, must understand the healthy boundaries you have set for yourself to bring your complete and productive self into the workplace. It's important to note that knowing your worth takes courage. In John C. Maxwell's book, *The 21 Indispensable Qualities of a Leader*, he states, "A courageous act often brings unexpected results." Have you ever been involved in negotiations on the price of an item that you really wanted—say it was shoes, iPad, TV, car, house, and whatever, and you went back and forth with the salesperson, and you finally got to the point of no return? The point where you were not willing to compromise on the price you were willing to pay for that item. You went into the negotiations with a clear idea of what you wanted and what you were willing to pay. In any case, you begin negotiations, and the salesperson presents an offer that is above what you are willing to pay, you counter with your offer, and they counter once again, asking for more. At some point, you have to decide what you are willing to compromise on.

In corporate America, when you are presented with a job opportunity, a company has a responsibility, and a right to do what is in their best interests, which, in most cases, is to offer at the market or competitive pay to attract and retain top talent. Those offers can either exceed candidates' expectations or, at times, be underwhelming as expectations may be higher. In the case of the latter, you must be firm in your conviction to know your worth and stick to it. There is a methodology in sales where every good salesman knows, "He or she who speaks first loses!" Think about it; you have already completed a successful interviewing process, demonstrated your experience, and shared your passion to the extent that this organization wants you, and they have extended a full-time job offer to you, where they are willing to welcome you into their organization with open arms.

Knowing your worth means

(1) you have done the market research to see what others in your field and area of expertise are getting paid;

(2) you have taken stock to understand what you have been paid in the past and the variance in pay for each position;

(3) you know what is being asked of you and the sweat equity it will require from you to get the job done effectively; and

(4) You always ask for more up front, whether it is a 20 percent increase in pay or more! You can be confident in what you're asking when

you are confident in your abilities and what you bring to the table.

It has taken me years to be comfortable in my own skin to develop a level of self-awareness and confidence to be able to negotiate; where I went into negotiation talks knowing my bottom line. I am proud of the progress I have made, and I realize that I have a long way to go. In this free agency game, there is always room for improvement.

CHAPTER 6

Keep the Bridges Intact!

*Discipline is the bridge between
goals and accomplishments!*

—Jim Rohn

*All of those who are around me are the bridge
to my success, so they are all important.*

—Manny Pacquiao

So you are realizing your full potential, you have entered this new space, and you are walking into your new season of opportunity. This is great, and I am excited for you; now it is time that you exercise the discipline to remember those who helped you get to where you are. There is no such thing as being self-made; in my humble opinion, that notion is ridiculous. Yes, it's true, and we earn certain accolades, awards, bonuses, and incentives based on our individual merit and/or work ethic. But a leader, CEO, owner, pastor, preacher, teacher, coach, father, mother, sister, brother, cousin, grandparent, manager, boss, mentor, or friend made an indelible impact upon your life to the extent that it changes the trajectory of your life. Someone poured into you at one time and said that you had the ability and skills to master the task that was laid out in front of you, and someone believed in you when you did not have the ability to believe in yourself. Even our negative circumstances can be used as fuel to propel us to the next level. People leave their imprint on our journey in a positive way or negative way; it really boils down to how we choose to view our past and growth because of it.

First, I encourage you to honor and recognize your past by making a list of those people that made a positive impact on your career. In this exercise, I want you to see the thread and imprint people have made from early on in your career to the present day— where someone put in a good word, someone referred you, or someone took a chance on you when others looked over your potential. George Shinn, the owner of the Charlotte Hornets, stated, "There is no such thing as a self-made man. You will reach goals only with the help of others."

Second, look to collaborate with others around you. So many people around you can offer you fresh ideas and if you are in sync with like-minded and goal-oriented people, opportunities are limitless. Your bridge should be filled with individuals that push you to reach your full potential and peers that encourage you not to settle for mediocrity. There is a quote that says, "You cannot change the people around you, but you can change the people you choose to be around." Surround yourself with people that push you toward greatness.

Third, build more bridges. Over the course of my career, I have learned that it is better to give than to receive. The more doors I help open for others, the more I have seen new opportunities flow my way as a result of my willingness to give. It is far better to give than to receive; my pastor and friend Kenneth Curry always says that, it is nice to be important, but it's more important to be nice. Do me a favor, people, un-ball that fist and open your hand; you see—now you are ready to receive the blessing God has Intended just for you.

Keep those bridges flowing both ways; you never know when you will need a helping hand.

CHAPTER 7

—⁓—

Work Harder

Dedication makes dreams come true.

—Kobe Bryant

For me, winning isn't something that happens suddenly on the field when the whistle blows and the crowds' roar. Winning is something that builds physically and mentally every day that you train and every night that you dream.

—Emmitt Smith

So you landed that dream job, or you have launched your business! You took that leap of faith shooting for the stars, and you have landed on the moon! Now what? It's time to take your foot off the gas, right? You have earned some rest and relaxation time, and it's time to take a much-needed break, right?

The answer is, maybe your situation allows you to take a breather. In most cases, however, we have chosen to take this leap of faith in advancing our careers, and it is now time to prove our worth. It is now time to prove that you belong. Dale Carnegie stated, "Do the hard jobs first. The easy jobs will take care of themselves." It's imperative that you take your work ethic to another level; you owe it to yourself to prove that you earned this opportunity based on merit and hard work.

Life is a gift, and each of us has an opportunity to change the trajectory of our lives. We can try new things and build legacies worth remembering; yes, generational wealth is important, but what is more important is that people remember how you treated them. How do people feel when they are in your presence? Have you paved the way for someone else to follow in your footsteps?

In John C. Maxwell's book *The 21 Indispensable Qualities of a Leader*, in chapter 10 titled "Initiative," he quotes Conrad Hilton, a hotel executive who states, "Success seems to be connected with action. Successful people keep moving. They make mistakes, but they don't quit." It's time to work harder, take initiative, plan, prepare, and execute your plan to maintain your new position. Create new habits and develop more stamina for the journey—venture into uncomfortable circles that will test your resolve and increase your faith. You have come this far; quitting is not an option.

CONCLUSION

—⁓⁓—

T hank you for taking the time to digest my words and thoughts. I hope and pray you have gained a new perspective and are energized to realize your full potential as a corporate free agent. The only thing holding you back at this point is you. *Corporate free agency* for some of you may mean you are to stay where you are currently and grow in maturity and knowledge. As I stated previously, you have the ability to master the content and skills in your respective field of professional endeavor; it's now time to put the plans into action and leverage this free agency period. You can do it; we can do it. You just have to be bold enough to believe.

ABOUT THE AUTHOR

Brandon Shelby was motivated to write *Corporate Free Agency: The 7 Principles Toward Career Ownership* from his many years and experiences working for numerous Fortune 500 firms. Shelby's desire is that through reading this book, readers will develop fresh perspectives, gain confidence, take ownership, and realize their full potential as corporate free agents.

Shelby's book delivers key moments like mastering the content and skills in your respective professional field, researching corporate opportunities, and putting plans into action to effectively leverage free agency opportunities.

He believes that hard work pays abundantly and that keeping the eye on the ball without the distraction of what others are doing is vital to personal growth and success.

Printed in the USA
CPSIA information can be obtained
at www.ICGtesting.com
LVHW051826110124
768548LV00071B/2963